I SCREAM,
YOU SCREAM,
WE ALL SCREAM FOR ICE CREAM

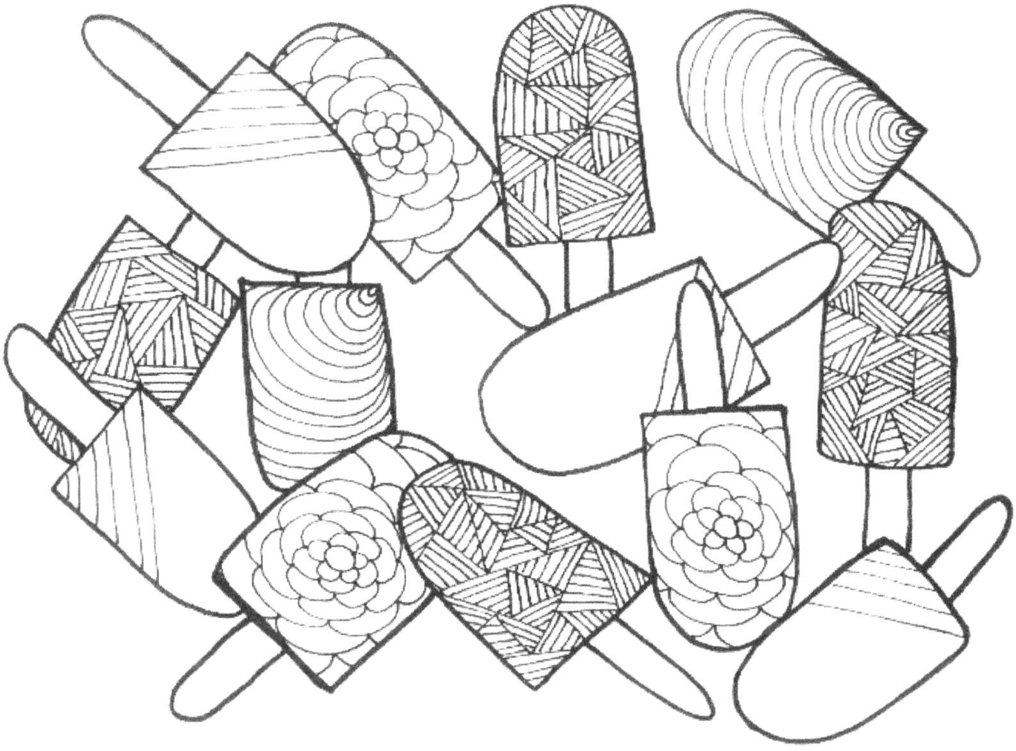

Coloring Book
By Rikki Franklin

Copyright ©2023

I SCREAM, YOU SCREAM, WE ALL SCREAM FOR ICE CREAM

Coloring Book

By
Rikki Franklin

Ever wished you could find a coloring book that combined the satisfyingly thick lines of a children's coloring book, the intricate details of adult coloring books, and a super fun, whimsical design?

Look no further! Let your imagination swirl with these ice cream-themed illustrations.

What are you waiting for? Let's get coloring!

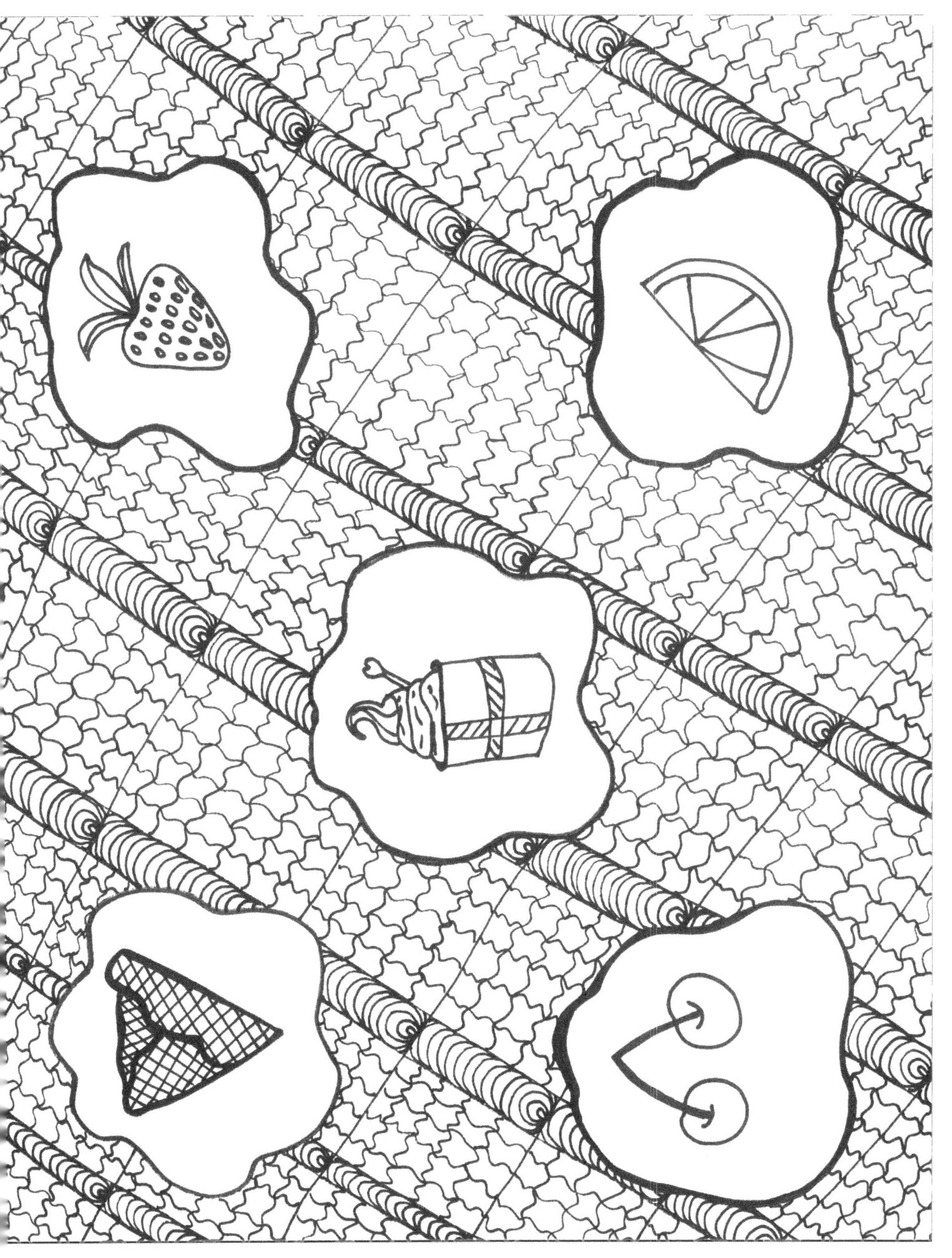

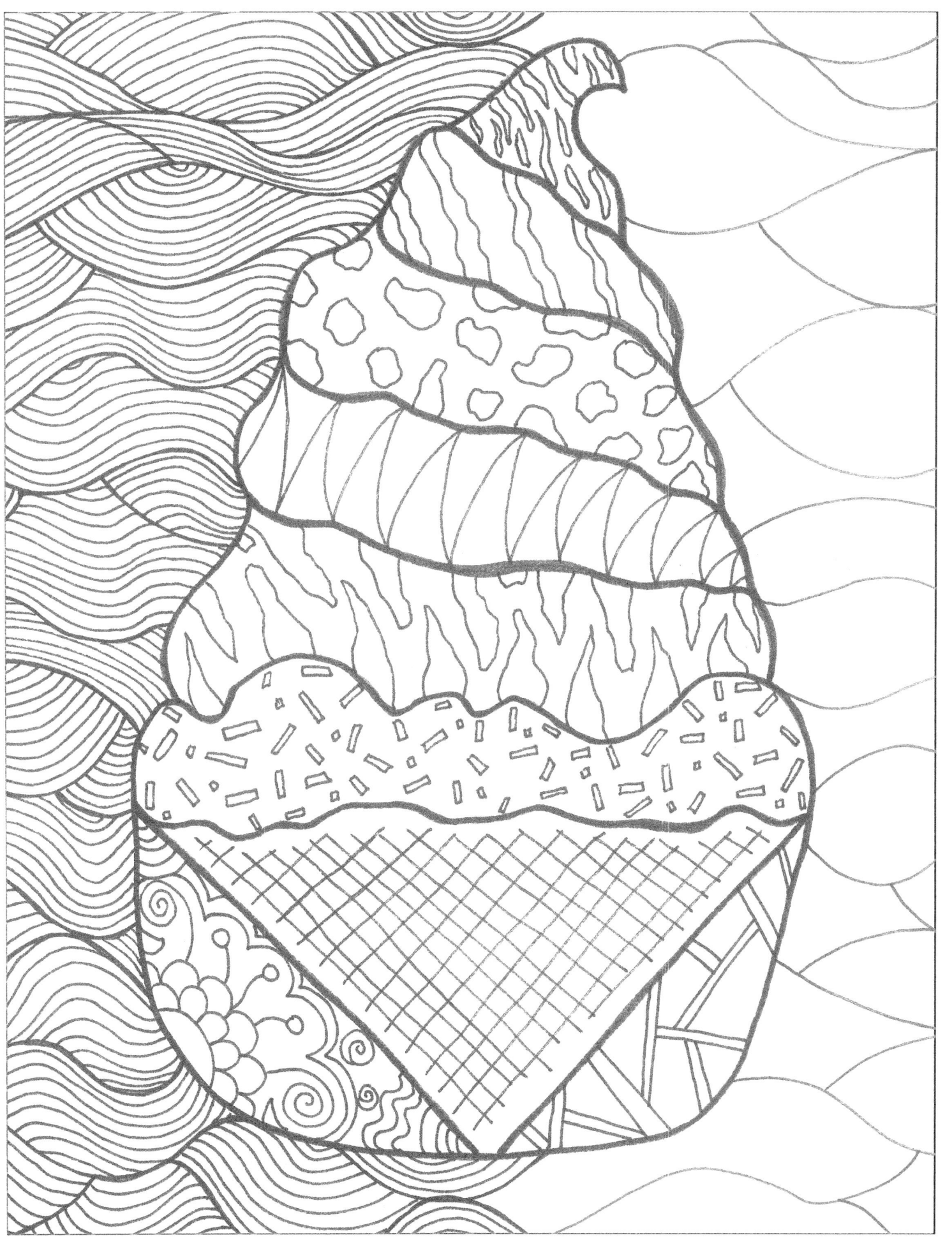

Made in United States
Orlando, FL
13 November 2023